God
Didn't Forget

God Didn't Forget Me

I'm Still Standing

Peggy Green

XULON PRESS

Xulon Press
2301 Lucien Way #415
Maitland, FL 32751
407.339.4217
www.xulonpress.com

© 2019 by Peggy Green

All rights reserved solely by the author. The author guarantees all contents are original and do not infringe upon the legal rights of any other person or work. No part of this book may be reproduced in any form without the permission of the author. The views expressed in this book are not necessarily those of the publisher.

Printed in the United States of America.

ISBN-13: 978-1-5456-7408-6

This book is being written in memory of all children, living or dead, who suffered from child abuse. This is my story. Hopefully someone will read this who will put a stop to child abuse.

I remember when I was two and I was the center of attention. I was the first child and grandchild locally. I was awakened when anyone came to visit because they were there to see me. Everybody seemed to love me. I had lots of pretty toys. When I woke up at night, Dad came to see about me. When I got up in the morning, Dad fixed my breakfast and dressed me. Dad had a deck of cards with letters and numbers on them. Braille was on the cards too. Mom and Dad were both completely blind.

Dad worked with me and I learned my letters so I could read the mail. They didn't like the neighbors all knowing their business. I was reading mail by the time I was four years old.

I am six now and I'm going to school today. Dad is ironing my dress and helps me to put it on. Dad ties my shoes because he can do it better than me. Dad puts the harness on Lady, his seeing eye dog. Together we walk to school.

They explained to me that eyes are like lightbulbs and theirs are out and do not work. Dad worked the light switch and turned the light on and off in an effort to show me about their eyes.

My first grade teacher is Mrs. Bell. She is really nice; however, my idea of school and hers are a little different. The first day of school, she got the class seated and quiet. I asked to go to the bathroom. When I came back, I peeked around the doorway and hollered, "Boo!". It took her a long time to get the class settled after that.

The boys in the class thought it was lots of fun to pull my sashes and tear my dresses. Dad told me to kick them and make them stop. I kicked a boy one day and broke his leg. After that, there were no more torn sashes.

One day Dad didn't come home from work. For many days he didn't come. I asked mom why and she said to "shut up". I soon learned they were getting something called a divorce. This is a strange new word I haven't heard before. I later wished I had never heard it.

We moved to a house on Harper Street. Mom would drink some stuff in a brown bottle and sleep all day. I have two brothers and a sister now. I go to school and when I come home I stand on a chair and cook supper. I also have to stand on a chair to iron my dress, but I can wash the dishes without standing on the chair.

I am seven years old now. Mom leaves at night in a taxi and is gone a long time. I take care of the kids by myself. Sometimes it is rough because they all cry at the same time. I turn on the radio and sing to them and a lot of times they stop crying. One brother is three years old, one is two, and my sister is one. When they are all asleep, I go to bed. Sometimes I get scared and just shake when it is real quiet.

When I was eight years old, a man came to the house with a suitcase and he stayed. "He" wasn't a nice man. "He" hollered and cussed a lot. "He" drank some stuff called beer and Mom did too.

We get to go to see Dad on the weekends and we have a good time. We go to the zoo and Dad has a television. We get to see The Lone Ranger and Tonto, Howdy Doody and Hopalong Cassidy. We go back to Mom's on Sunday afternoon. We cry and beg not to go back.

The stepfather has started whipping us a lot. At Mom's we have to line up and "he" searches us. Any candy, money, or toys is taken away. I started putting dimes inside my jaw so I could use the phone to call Dad.

Mom sends me to the store for a large Hershey bar. She sits in her chair and eats it all. We begged for some candy and she hits us and hollers, "Go away!". "He" checks the house and talks to her when he gets home from work. He come in and hits me. Mom sits in her chair and calls sister and baby brother to her. As soon as her fingers touch them, she pinches the skin and twists it really hard. Big brother is getting smart; he doesn't come anymore.

I was standing on the chair cooking one day and "he" hit me and made the pan of food spill on the floor. Then "he" really got mad and started beating me with the strap off his saddle. The floor was slippery and I fell down and he kept hitting me. I never knew why he was hitting me. We would be sitting at the table eating and "he" would just hit us, knock our chair over, and we would fall to the floor. "He" never said why.

Mom said I have to stay home from school today. I don't know why, but I have learned not to ask questions. She tells me to come out in the yard. We are standing in the front yard. The big bus stops down at the corner. "He" gets off the bus. Mom asks me if there is a woman with him and I said "no". All of a sudden both of her hands are around my throat and I feel myself falling down. I fight and try to get her hands off me. I can't breathe. Everything goes black.

I woke up and two policemen were standing over me. They asked me if I was alright. I had to go in the house. I was so ashamed, I had wet my pants. Mom and "him" talked to the policemen for a long time and they went away. I stayed home for a long time until the bruises went away.

I am 10 years old now. Mom said I have to stay home again and did not say why. A man with a black bag comes to the house and goes into Mom's bedroom. The door is shut. He leaves a few minutes later. About 3pm, Mom is going to the bathroom and she calls me to come. She falls down on the floor and starts hollering, "Pull it out!" I do and I see a lot of blood and large messy thing between her legs. I pull it away from her and she grabs a string-like thing and chews it apart. She screams to throw it in the commode, but it is too big, so I throw a wash rag in the water and flush the pot. I look at the bloody thing and decide it is a baby. I wrap it in a towel and push it around behind the toilet. Mom goes back to bed and the man with the black bag comes back. I point where the messy thing is and he takes it away.

Mom tells us we have to go live in a children's home for a while. All our clothes are packed. We go in a car. We see a sign that says "All Church Home". We are taken to a big room upstairs with lots of beds in rows. My sister and I go to the girls ward. My two brothers go to the boys ward. They take all our clothes away and give us other clothes to wear. Grandma had given me a pretty coat with a fuzzy collar for Christmas. One day, I saw another girl wearing my coat. I tried to take it away from her and Mrs. R., the head lady, whipped me and said it wasn't my coat anymore. Lots of things aren't the same anymore. The food is terrible. A big, fat lady with no shoes, does the cooking and we don't go to the same school.

Both of my brothers wear glasses and can barely see without them. The kids at school take their glasses off and hold them over their heads, dance around, and tease them. I have to beat them up and get the glasses back. I sure am getting tired of all this fighting, but I'm getting good at it. We take a sack lunch everyday and the bologna is always green. I take it out and eat the bread. We get two cookies and an apple or banana. I showed my bologna sandwich to the principal and he called the home and chewed them out. I got a whipping when I came in from school.

I finally get tired of this place and take a hike. I run into a big river that looks deep and I can't swim. I guess I have to get back. We walk past a bakery every day and it smells so good. I sure would like to eat there. They are always telling me I need to make a lot of changes, but nobody else has to make changes.

I heard my brother crying one night. It was real late. I went to the boys ward and the woman was beating my younger brother. He was lying on the floor, bleeding from the mouth and nose. She just kept hitting him over and over. I jumped on her and fought for the strap. I started screaming and another woman came in and broke us up. I picked up my brother, cleaned him up, and took him to my bed. Sister never would sleep in her bed, she always slept in mine. Now there are three in my bed. A woman told me I couldn't do that and I told her to go to hell. The next day I told the head lady there were big beer bottles under the matron's bed. They fired her and she left.

Mom came and got us today. I really don't want to go home, but I don't want to stay here either. We're moving now. This house is on Griggs Street and is bigger. "He" is still here and has even more fits now. Every morning starts the same. "He" comes in our room, pulls the cover off of us, and starts whipping us. It is a hell of a way to wake up!

Mom came home from the hospital today with a new baby. It is a little girl and she is cute. Mom still drinks the stuff in the brown bottle and sleeps all day. The baby wets and dirties her diaper all day, and is never changed until I come home from school. The sheet and carpet both smell like pee and they always gripe about the smell. I don't know how to get it out.

The whippings are almost everyday now. There is no way to do enough to stay out of trouble. Sometimes I am so tired when I go to bed, I don't know if I can get up tomorrow, but the strap always wakes me up.

Mom says she is going to have another baby. We have so many kids around here now, I don't know what I'll do with another one. I still tell Dad about everything and he keeps saying, "I'm trying to get you out of there".

For several years now, I have been telling the principal when I get beat. He calls a lady and she strips me, looks at the marks, and takes pictures. I miss so many days at school and my grades are low, but the teachers always pass me. I can run real fast and I've done good on the track team. I got a school letter for the volleyball team.

In the 7th grade, a girl cussed me in Spanish in the bathroom. She was waiting for me after school with a knife in her hand. I kicked her in the stomach and knocked her out, then ran and jumped on the bus to go home.

Mom had the baby today but they didn't bring it home. It died. Mom said it was deformed. Mom locked all the screen doors so "he" couldn't get in. He broke in and mom told him I did it. "He" said he was going to beat the hell out of me, so I took off running down the street. "He" chased me two blocks before he caught me. "He" whipped me in the street with all the neighbors watching. Everybody is afraid to call the police.

One of brothers accidentally dropped his comic book on the floor. "He" demanded to know whose it was. Neither of the boys would confess. "He" decided it belonged to my older brother. The whipping started and brother refused to cry. "He" got mad. I realized brother was in danger, so I jumped in and tried to make him stop. "He" grabbed me and threw me out the back door and locked it. "He" went back to beating brother and after "he" let me in, I found my brother lying in his bed. He was very white, bruised all over, and had a big knot on the side of his head. I couldn't wake him up. He laid in his bed for two days. He soiled the bed and I clean him and the bed until he woke up.

Mom has been letting us got to church some Sundays, but I don't know too much about this God fella. I go to my room, get on my knees and ask him not to let my brother die. I am really scared. Things seem to be going from bad to worse. The judge and the courts seem to be so slow.

One day a neighbor offered mom a registered German Shepherd puppy. "He" said he was not feeding two dogs; we already had a puppy named Prissy. My little sister had been locked out of the house for years, so she stayed in the dog house and spent a lot of time with Prissy. "He" tied Prissy up to the clothesline pole and made us line up really close. "He" took a board and started to beat Prissy. We all jumped in and tried to make him stop. "He" beat Prissy to death. We were all bruised and bloody. "He" went in the house and went to bed. I was ordered to bury the dog and I did. I took my two brothers and one sister in the house and bathed all three and put them to bed. I got to bed at 1am.

One evening "he" tried to make me kiss him on the mouth. I refused. "He" got mad and got the strap. "He" started whipping me and I got mad. I kicked him in the balls; "he" hit me with his hand; I punched him in the nose and knocked his glasses off; "he" hit me with his fist and I hit my head on the commode tank. I fell in the floor and all was quiet. I woke up later in my bed, my clothes still on. Two days later, I noticed feeling swollen in the groin area. I really don't know if I was kicked or what happened. I started wondering, what was going to happen next. My dad was the only person I told that "he" tried to kiss me; I was afraid to tell him more.

I started smuggling more dimes in my jaw so I could call Dad whenever I needed to. Dad told me that Grandad paid a man to tell him if "he" touched one of us again. If he did, he would die.

Mom brought home another baby today. Now I really have my hands full. Five kids, plus me, Mom, and "him". Nobody does any cooking, cleaning, or ironing except me. Mom sleeps all day, every day. Mom and "him" fight all the time. They get loud and the new baby cries a lot.

I go to their bedroom to see what was wrong. "He" had a gun and said he was going to shoot her. She is fighting him for the pistol. I jump in and reach for the pistol and we all three roll off the bed onto the floor still holding on. Both of them are drunk and I somehow get a hold of the gun. I have never touched a gun. I don't know how to use one. I hide the gun under a big chair and they both go to sleep. The next day, I am ordered to give him the gun. I refuse. He beats me and I continue to refuse.

A couple months later, I was running from one kid to another trying to take care of everyone, while also cooking a pot of beans. The beans scorched. "He" came home from work and told me I would get a whipping later. After I finished supper and the dishes, here "he" comes. "He" beats me until both my legs are bleeding. I am shaking so bad I can't unbutton my clothes. I lay across my bed and try to think. I ache and burn all over. I have had enough. I can't take anymore. I am afraid someone will wind up dead.

I unfasten my window screen and climb out with dimes in my jaw. I go to a payphone and call Dad. He comes in a taxi and takes me to the hospital for treatment. I am thirteen years old. The doctor talks to the police, the police talk to the sheriff, and the judge is awakened. By 9:00am the next day, the custody was changed. We finally get to live with Dad!

We have been living in this hell for seven years. I broke the law by running away. I was sworn in at court and took the stand. "He" jumped up and yelled, "if you say one word, I will kill you!". I laughed as the bailiff handcuffed him. They removed him from the court and he was given 30 days in jail for child abuse. He served 24 hours. Our dad requested he be released so his family would not go hungry.

The judge explained that I was now a juvenile because I ran away. I told him if he had been beat like I was, he would have run away too. He ordered me to go home with my mom for two weeks and pack up the kids clothes. I refused. I told the judge I would go to jail before I would go back there. I felt like I had nothing to lose. I had fought all my life, became a criminal trying to save our lives, and the whole court had heard the death threat from the stepfather. I remembered Mom choking me and I knew she would kill me while I slept.

We went in two weeks to pick up the other three kids. The two boys were sitting on the porch. No little sister. Mom had escaped to the port of Houston and boarded a ship for South America. The sheriff called the FBI and a woman agent boarded the ship and took my sister out of my mom's arms. We went to live with Dad and our grandparents. We all had malnutrition and anemia.

Grandma cooked all the time and we ate until we got full and vomited many times until our stomachs were used to the food. There were no more beatings. Everyone was kind to us. Granddad started secretly teaching me to drive. We had a lot of fun. He used to take me with him on his job and we drove all over the city.

I turned fourteen in June and I got to go to summer camp. I had fun until about the third day. I woke up that morning and there was blood all over my bed. I was scared and knew I was dying. I pulled the covers over my head and cried. My counselor talked to me and called Dad. She helped me get cleaned up and got me all the stuff I needed to deal with the menses.

I got my first driver's license at fourteen. At our moms, our food was severely restricted. When I went to the grocery store, I would steal a package of cupcakes. We would meet on the side of the house when I got home and split the two cakes four ways. I didn't have to steal anymore. I drove Dad to work, went to school, and helped out around the house.

One day Granddad started forgetting things. He got weak and sick. He had surgery and we were told he was riddled with cancer. We cared for him at home and he got thinner and thinner and smaller and smaller by the day. He was a very nice man, loved us, and helped us in any way he could. I was asked to take the kids to the Stock Show one evening in February 1961. Dad didn't want the little kids to be there when Granddad died.

When we returned home, I was told Grandad was asking for me. I went in to see him and he told me he loved me and to "go on being the sweet girl you've always been". He died holding my hand. It took three men to break his grip after he died. I loved him so much and feel like he was trying to take me with him. I miss him so much still and to this day, I cannot think about him without crying.

I was still in High School and struggling with my grades. I started going to school an hour early so the student tutor could help me. I had a boyfriend and we had been dating for some time. We both went to the Baptist church. I decided to join the church and accept Christ as my savior. My family is mostly Methodist and were very upset when I made my choice. I believe I was baptized in 1962 and Grandma and Dad refused to attend. My little sister asked to come and she was the only family present for my baptism. I was told by my Grandma, "I guess you're going to be the black sheep of the family." I was hurt and didn't understand why different was bad. I didn't feel bad or different; I felt like I was doing the right thing for my life.

I struggled until I graduated in 1963 with a B average. I had considered quitting at one time and Dad told me he would escort me to school with his guide dog if I did. I would have been so embarrassed, I decided to stay in school. I am glad I did.

We bought a new Ford Station Wagon in 1963. We went on a vacation to Austin, San Antonio, and Padre Island. We camped out all the way across Texas and back home; just four kids, a blind man, and a guide dog. No weapons needed. We had some scary times and a lot of good times.

Dad's dog, "Chica" saved our lives when a motorcycle gang surrounded us in a state park. We were driving down a highway one day and little sister said,

"Gee Dad, look! Piggyback cows!" I almost ran the car off the road laughing so hard. I got a bad sunburn on Padre Island. We met lots of new people. A blind woman we stayed with one night, was horrified to discover me rolling my hair in the dark. I told her, I do it all the time; you learn to adapt. We returned safe and sound after two weeks.

I turned 18 when we got back home. Dad had always told me I could make my own decisions when I turned 18. I took my savings and bought my own car. Dad got mad and said I had no right to do that. I also decided it was time to come and go as I saw fit. Dad didn't like that either. He wanted me to continue under his rules because I was an "example for the other three kids". I have been taking care of this family since I was six years old, I have met every challenge, and I have cleared my probation. I felt like I was not being allowed to grow up or mature because of the other kids.

One evening I told them I was going to my boyfriends house to watch TV. Dad said I wasn't and Grandma started quoting the Bible and hollering. Dad came in my room and blocked the doorway. We argued, then he pushed me back and pinned me to the bed. I got scared and started screaming. I had never seen him act like that.

The neighbors called the police and Grandma called her preacher. The police came and pulled Dad off of me. They told Dad he had overstepped his bounds. I called my preacher. Both pastors told Grandma she was quoting the Bible to say what she wanted it to say. I made the decision to leave. The police stayed until I got all my things in my car. I was thoroughly confused and bewildered. I felt all alone and scared. It wasn't the first time.

I went to my uncle's house and spent the night. We talked about what happened and he just shook his head. I lived with some friends for one month then I moved to the YWCA for a while. I had a hard time finding work. I finally got a steady job and moved into an apartment.

One day the gas oven blew up in my face. I got third degree burns on my hands, arms, and face. All of hair fell off. My boyfriend had started drinking heavily and I refused to see him.

I started dating another man and I really liked him. I got pregnant and we married. He sold my car and TV, we started to argue a lot and had a lot of problems with his family. He had bad headaches and got violent more often. A son was born and was a big healthy boy.

One day when the baby was two weeks old, I caught my husband trying to smother him with a blanket. I grabbed a knife and chased him out the door. He returned with his parents, and we decided to try again. The next time he tried to smother the baby, I screamed and the neighbor man shot at him with a pistol. I agreed to try again and stayed close to the baby. The baby rode in many laundry baskets. We moved to a small house. One night my husband said he was going to get cigarettes.

He returned two weeks later to tell me he left me. I filed for a divorce.

I went job hunting and found a job making 85 cents per hour. I hired a babysitter, worked and lived on peanut butter sandwiches for a long time. I could buy all the food and medicine the baby needed. I washed his diapers out by hand. I put him in his stroller and we walked everywhere for a year.

I had been having a prowler at night. I didn't know who it was. The shoe size was different from my ex-husband. I had no telephone, TV, or radio. I had no weapon for protection. I had to wait until daylight to call the police. They advised me to get a gun. I borrowed a .22 caliber rifle and two shells. I loaded it and kept it loaded. The baby was three months old.

One night I raised the blinds on the bathroom window. There was a mans face pressed against the glass. I wet my pants. There was a butcher knife on the ledge. I grabbed the rifle and ran to the back door, jerked it open, raised the gun and fired. The first time in my life to shoot a gun. I shot the prowler on the inside of my six foot white picket fence. I grabbed the baby and gun, and ran to the neighbors house to use the phone. The police came and we made a report. We followed the trail of blood for one half block down the alley to the street. He had got in a car and got away. He had already removed the window screen, all the boards around the window, and was trying to pry the window open. It was locked on the inside. The police gave me all his tools. They never found him. I never had any more prowlers. I still use that butcher knife when I cut up a chicken today.

I waited several weeks to tell dad about the prowler. He asked me to move in the garage apartment behind their house, so I did. Before I moved, Dad came to my house with my older brother. They saw that I had only bread and peanut butter in my kitchen. I had lost a lot of weight while I was "roughing" it.

A friend sold me a 1949 Plymouth and we had wheels again. I started dating some and I met the man that would become my second husband. We were married in 1966. He had a house in the country and I had some furniture. The baby was one and a half years old. We had a lot of fun and only ever argued about the kids. He had three kids from his first wife. I got pregnant in 1968 and our daughter was born in 1969.

She was small but healthy. When she was fourteen months old, she got sick. She went to the hospital having seizures and they diagnosed her with a parasitic virus. Only three cases had ever been reported to the state. They said she would grow out of it or it would develop into another disease. She took a lot of medication and had multiple tests, and at age seven, it disappeared.

My husband worked on cars for people and one day my best friend's T-Bird had broken down. My husband had it up on blocks in the garage. He always hollers for me to bring him coffee or a cigar. Suddenly, he calls, "Honey! Honey! Come here quick!". I went to the garage and saw the car had fallen off the blocks and his left arm was pinned to the cement floor. "Get this damn thing off me!". I grabbed the bumper and lifted and pushed all at the same time. The car rolled off his arm. He rubbed it and decided it would be alright. This was all before 911.

My husband had always worked two jobs since before we were married. His kids come over on the weekends and we go fishing, camping, or to the drive-in movie. Sometimes he cries worrying about the kids. I have to drive them home many times because he just can't do it.

I remember crying when we left our Dad. Sometimes he had to pull us out of the car, take us to the door, and push us in the house. Dad would always tell me, "You have to go back. Be a big girl.". If he only knew how small I felt. I wondered if I would ever be a big girl. I understood what my husband was going through. I helped him all I could. At one point, my husband's son came to live with us. He stayed for a year and three months then he went back to live with his mom and sisters.

In April 1977, my grandma is in the nursing home and expected to pass away at any time. On April 3rd, 4th, and 5th, I keep having a reoccuring dream: The phone rings, I answer it and a man is screaming, "He's dead! He's dead! My God, he's dead!". My grandma peacefully passed away on April 6th at 9:00pm. April 7th was Good Friday and we were having Easter parties at school. My son and I got home at 5:30pm and the phone was ringing. I answered and my dream was now real. "He's dead! He's dead! My god, he's dead!". My brother in law had been killed in a bulldozer accident. His funeral was on Easter Sunday. Grandma's was on Monday.

The week following the funerals, I had a different dream. For three nights in a row, I saw my maternal grandma's face. She's talking, yet there is no sound. I called Dad and told him. He called back and said she had died on the day his mother was buried. My mom had never called to tell me. I considered my dream a gift from God. I would not have known for a very long time if not for the dream.

All the kids grow up. Some get married and start having families of their own. In 1980, my husband and I decided to be foster parents. It seems like I just can't do enough for the world. We trained and were called to take a set of twins. They were two months old, a boy and a girl, and had beautiful chocolate skin. Many of neighbors had given personal references for us, but now they wanted to burn our house down.

Soon a neighbor called and told us the KKK was watching us. We noticed a man in car would come after my husband went to work. He would park in the road in front of our house. I called the sheriff and he drove off. I got tired of it and one day I put all the kids in the walk in closet and told them not to open the door for anyone but me. I went out the back door with a 12 gauge shotgun. I ran down the drive with the gun aimed at the car and screamed at the top of my lungs. The man turned the car broadside in the road, left and never returned. I went back in the house and all the kids were fine. Shortly after, the twins were moved to another foster home. They stayed with us for only four months.

Next we got a one year old boy who was born mentally retarded. He was a challenge and kept us busy. After him, we got a fourteen year old girl. She was a moving challenge. During that time, my mother in law had a stroke and my father in law had a heart attack at the same time. The girl was moved soon after. We were busy hospital and nursing home sitting until my father in law passed away.

In 1982, my husband was 44 and I was 37. He told me we needed to talk so we sat down at the kitchen table. He told me he was confused and mixed up and didn't know if he wanted to be married anymore. I asked him what was wrong and he didn't know. He say he wanted to be a park ranger and decided to stay. I feared losing my marriage and having no way to earn a living. I decided to go back to school. I sold my cow and bought uniforms and books. I earned my LVN license and took a job with the hospital.

One day, I had another dream. The phone rang and voice said my mother had died. Three days later my mom called. I had not heard from her in 30 years. I answered her questions and was honest about how I felt. She asked me to come and see her. She had nine kids and only one daughter came to see her. She did not understand why. I told her she had disowned me 21 years ago, but she didn't remember that.

In the following two years, we talked on the phone and I sent cards. I worked full time and I worried about my daughter. She was having some emotional problems. I do a lot more praying and look forward to vacation. On May 30th, my son goes for surgery on his back, then June 11th my mother in law has surgery.

August 16th, 1986, my husband I went to visit my husband's friend in the hospital in Grand Prairie. A lady hit us in the side of our car and my husband gets knocked out. Our car is wrecked. We have to take a taxi back home and my husband has a knot on the side of his head. My aunt and uncle give me a poem:

> We take a bump today, another bump tomorrow. But as we bump from hump to hump, we are sure to borrow, a lot of fun along the way. So get across the rough, and before long you'll find, you left behind the road you thought was tough.
>
> Author Unknown

The bumps continue to come as I grow older. Son has another back surgery. Cousin takes treatments for cancer. Cousin passed away. A man hits my car from behind on the highway. Totals the car and my back. I have three surgeries to fix my back and have to retire from nursing because it is no longer safe for me to lift. I get diabetes, osteoporosis, have an aneurysm, occluded arteries, and calcium deposits on my spine. Mom, Dad, and stepmom all pass away in 1993. Husband is diagnosed with asbestos poisoning in 2006. He worked for his company for 43 years with a perfect safety record. My younger brother dies from cancer in 2012. I have open heart surgery in 2016.

My husband and I were married 50 years in December 2016. We spent all of our married life rebuilding, mowing, and weed eating three cemeteries. He passed away in 2017. His last MRI showed he had three strokes during his life. He was a good man. He never hit or cussed me. He provided for me. The kids have also been great. It's a lonely life now without him, but God didn't forget about me. I'm still standing.

www.ingramcontent.com/pod-product-compliance
Ingram Content Group UK Ltd.
Pitfield, Milton Keynes, MK11 3LW, UK
UKHW022211230426
12048UKWH00016BA/778